THE WEAPONS ENCYCLOPÆDIA
TANK AIRCRAFT AFV SHIP ARTILLERY VEHICLES SECRET WEAPON

TWE-015 ENG

ITALIAN ARTILLERY 1914-1945

THE WEAPONS ENCYCLOPAEDIA

EDITORIAL STAFF
Luca Cristini, Paolo Crippa.

ACADEMIC EDITORIAL STAFF
Enrico Acerbi, Massimiliano Afiero, Aldo Antonicelli, Ruggero Calò, Luigi Carretta, Flavio Chistè, Anna Cristini, Carlo Cucut, Salvo Fagone, Enrico Finazzer, Björn Huber, Andrea Lombardi, Aymeric Lopez, Marco Lucchetti, Luigi Manes, Giovanni Maressi, Francesco Mattesini, Federico Peirani, Alberto Peruffo, Maurizio Raggi, Andrea Alberto Tallillo, Antonio Tallillo, Massimo Zorza.

PUBLISHED BY
Luca Cristini Editore (Soldiershop), via Orio, 33/D - 24050 Zanica (BG) ITALY.

MAIN DISTRIBUTORS
Soldiershop - www.soldiershop.com, Amazon, Ingram Spark, Berliner Zinnfigurem (D), LaFeltrinelli, Mondadori, Libera Editorial (Spain), Google book (eBook), Kobo, (eBoook), Apple Book (eBook).

PUBLISHING'S NOTES
All rights reserved. No part of this publication may be reproduced, stored in a retrieval system, or transmitted, in any form, or by any means, electronic, mechanical, photocopying, recording or otherwise, without the express written consent of Luca Cristini Editore (already Soldiershop.com). Luca Cristini Editore has made every reasonable effort to locate, contact and acknowledge rights holders and to correctly apply terms and conditions to Content. Every reasonable effort has been made to trace copyright holders and to obtain their permission for the use of copyright material. The author and publisher apologize for any errors or omissions in this work, and would be grateful if notified of any corrections that should be incorporated in future reprints or editions of this book.

LICENSES COMMONS
This book may utilize part of material marked with license creative commons 3.0 or 4.0 (CC BY 4.0), (CC BY-ND 4.0), (CC BY-SA 4.0) or (CC0 1.0). We give appropriate attribution credit and indicate if change were made in the acknowledgments field. Our WTW books series utilize only fonts licensed under the SIL Open Font License or other free use license.

CONTRIBUTORS TO THIS VOLUME
We would like to thank the main contributors to this issue: Enrico Finazzer and Carlo Cucut. The profiles of the floats are all by the author. The colouring of the photos is by Anna Cristini. Special thanks to national and/or private institutions such as: Army General Staff, State Archives, Bundesarchiv, Nara, Library of Congress, Wikipedia, USAF, etc. To P.Crippa, A.Lopez, L.Manes, C.Cucut, Tallillo archives. etc. for having made available images or other items from their archives.

For details of other military history titles published or download a free pdf catalogue, or for every information visit our website: www.soldiershop.com or www.cristinieditore.com. E-mail: info@soldiershop.com. Keep up to date on Facebook & Twitter: https://www.facebook.com/soldiershop.publishing

Title: **ITALIAN ARTILLERY 1914-1945 VOL. 2** Code.: **TWE-015 EN**
Series by L. S. Cristini
ISBN code: 9791255890102. First edition September 2023
THE WEAPONS ENCICLOPAEDIA (SOLDIERSHOP) is a trademark of Luca Cristini Editore.

THE WEAPONS ENCYCLOPÆDIA
TANK AIRCRAFT AFV SHIP ARTILLERY VEHICLES SECRET WEAPON

ITALIAN ARTILLERY 1914-1945 Vol. 2

100/22, 104/32, 149/12, 149/35, 152/37, M210, M240, M260/90, M305
OM 36DM TRACTORS, FIAT 708, BREDA 32

LUCA STEFANO CRISTINI

BOOK SERIES FOR MODELERS & COLLECTORS

CONTENTS

Introduction 5

Cannons inherited from the Great War 5
- -100/22 howitzer 7
- -104 cannon then 105/32 15
- -149/12 howitzer mod. 14 19
- -149/35 cannon mod. 1901 25
- -152/37 howitzer 31
- -210/8 D.S. mortar 39
- -240 bombard 43
- -260/9 mortar mod. 16 47
- -305/17 mortar 51

Trucks and tractors 55
- -OM autocarretta 55
- -FIAT 708 tractor 57

Bibliography 58

▲ A 149/35 piece preserved in Redipuglia.

INTRODUCTION

Following the first volume on Italian cannons, in this second part we will treat and complete the study and analysis of artillery pieces inherited from the First World War, both domestically produced and sources of war prey (typically Austro-Hungarian) following the victory in 1915-18.

The criterion used will still be that of the growing calibre, i.e. from light pieces onwards. With the third volume, which will complete our work on Italian artillery in the first fifty years of the twentieth century, we will mainly deal with the more modern types of artillery, designed from the second half of the 1930s. From this volume we will also expressly discuss the bombards in use in those years, while tractors will be distributed in various ways throughout the three volumes in preferably chronological order.

In this second volume, we will deal with the following artillery pieces and artillery vehicles:
- **The 100/22 howitzer 17 Mod. 1914-1919.** Born as Skoda 10 houfnive vz 14/19;
- **The 105/32 Mod. 1915 cannon.** 104/32 former Austrian, from 1938 105/32 with Italian modifications;
- **The 149/12 Mod. 1914 cannon.** Krupp Germany, and produced under licence by Ansaldo and Vickers-Terni;
- **The 149/35 Mod. 1901 cannon.** Production Royal Army Arsenal of Turin ARET;
- **The 152/37-105/28 howitzer Mod. 1916.** Produced by the Austrian Skoda;
- **The 210/8 D.S. mortar** manufactured by Ansaldo in 1900;
- **The 240/12 bombard.** Designed in France (mortier de 240) and later in Italy by Vickers-Terni;
- **The 260/9 mortar Mod. 16** Designed by the French company Schneider, then made in Italy under licence.
- **The 305/17 mortar** manufactured by Ansaldo in 1900.

A number of artillery tractors are included in the appendix.
- **Autocarretta OM Mod. 1932.** Light artillery auxiliary tractor;
- **Fiat-Oci 708 CM model 19135 tractor.** Nationally produced artillery tractor.

▲ Beautiful picture of a 100/22 cannon kept at the War Museum in Athens, Greece.

100/22 HOWITZER WITH PROTECTIVE SHIELD - SPANISH CIVIL WAR 1936-1939

100/22 HOWITZER

Having lost the war, Austria also had to give up many regions, among them the new Czechoslovakia, and with it their best-known and most sophisticated armament factory, Škoda. At the end of the conflict, partly to help the economy of the new nation, Škoda resumed production for the Czechoslovak army of the Vz. 1914 . The Plzeň industry immediately set about modernising the piece: the main improvement concerned the barrel, which was increased from 19 to 24 calibres, effectively turning the howitzer into a cannon. This made the weapon much more modern and high-performance, especially in terms of range. The new weapon, named Škoda houfnice vz 14/19, was very successful throughout Europe and was produced for the country and for export until 1939 in several thousand units. In the Czechoslovakian army, the piece was immediately the campaign standard. In Europe, the cannon was sold to Hungary, Poland and the Kingdom of Yugoslavia; it soon became one of the most popular pieces in the armies of Central Europe. Purchasers then also included Greece, while the Kingdom of Italy, which already possessed thousands of 100/17 Mod. 14s as wartime prey, experimented with replacing the barrel with that of the vz. 14/19, which, however, did not meet with the approval of our military engineers.

With the occupation of Czechoslovakia, all national pieces were then requisitioned by the Wehrmacht and were extensively employed in the French campaign of May-June 1940 and in the initial stages of the invasion of the Soviet Union in 1941. It was then gradually withdrawn from the front line and relegated to fixed positions in the Atlantic Wall, where it was employed until the end of the war.

With Italy's entry into the war in May 1940, their German allies ceded some of the pieces to the Regio Esercito, which ended up being used mainly by the CSIR on the Russian front. In Italy, the piece was named the **100/22 17 Mod. 14/19 howitzer**. As it was entirely similar to the 100/17 already described in the first volume, we refer you to those notes as well. The main difference was the slightly elongated muzzle.

The highly versatile piece was used on all war fronts; it was certainly present during the Spanish Civil War that began in 1936. It later played a role on the World War II fronts mainly as a position piece in Europe and North Africa.

▲ The 100/22 howitzer on an elastic cart pulled by a Pavesi P4. Courtesy by Enrico Finazzer.

100/22 HOWITZER SAND CAMOUFLAGE - NORTH AFRICAN WAR 1940-1943

TECHNICAL DATA:	
Entry into service	1919
Weight in battery	1.430 kg
Bullet weight	11,45 kg
Initial projectile speed	415 m/sec
Piece length	5,80 m
Vertical firing range	-8° / +20°
Maximum range	9.600 m
Rate of fire	min 4 / max 6 per minute
Number of pieces available in 1940	406

By contrast, an entirely different use was made in Sicily, where at least three batteries were made mobile in order to better counter Allied landing operations in the south of the island. Some of these pieces were later captured by the British, who subjected them to technical tests.

It should also be remembered that the majority of the pieces available to the Italian army came, as mentioned, from various sources. Among these, one of the most conspicuous (about sixty or so) came from the collapse of the Yugoslav army in 1940. A large part of these weapons were employed and framed in at least 13 artillery regiments in infantry divisions during all the operations in the Balkans until the fighting against Tito's partisans.

In total, the royal army possessed just over 400 such pieces. Over 350 were animal-drawn and the rest mechanically driven. Almost all of the latter were at the disposal of the Ariete II armoured division. Other howitzers of this type were sent to guard the coasts of Sardinia as well as Sicily.

▲ The Czech cannon was also acquired by the Poles. Here we see a hippotrained battery destroyed by German fire in the first weeks of the campaign in September 1939.

100/22 HOWITZER WITH PROTECTIVE SHIELD - EUROPEAN THEATRE 1940-1945

The armistice of September 1943 and the ensuing defence of Rome by the Italian army saw the participation of our howitzer, intent on trying in every way to curb the powerful German offensive on the capital. Already towards the end of the month, again in 1943, in San Pietro Vernotico, near Brindisi, the first motorised grouping of the Regio Esercito was formed, freshly allied (co-belligerent), which fought against the former allies for the first time, taking part in the Battle of Monte Lungo. On that occasion, 100/22 howitzers were used again.

As is well known, at the time Italy was divided in two: in the South with the Savoy in the 1st Motorised Corps and in the North within the newly formed RSI led by Mussolini.

It follows that these howitzers were also used in parallel by the army of the Italian Social Republic. Two batteries belonging to the 10th Marine Infantry Division were equipped with them; this unit fought with the Allies at Anzio and later participated in the defence of the Gothic Line.

TECHNICAL FEATURES

The muzzle and muzzle are the same as those of the country Mod. 14. The muzzle was on a steel body (barrel), fitted with 3 additional hoops with paw guides for sliding on the smoothbore, supported directly by the cradle. This contained the hydro-pneumatic rotating sleeve firing brake with spring-loaded retriever. The tracks were protected from dust and other dirt with strips of sheet metal initiated at the rims. The locking mechanism was provided by a horizontally sliding wedge-shaped bolt with semi-automatic quick action that ensured closure by the brass case of the firing charge. The muzzle was single-tailed, open in the centre to allow recoil at high firing angles; a plate was fixed to the muzzle head on which the slide was hinged. The shaft was connected to the hall that carried 12-spoke wooden wheels, 130 cm in diameter. These, in the 1930s, were partially replaced on some parts by metal wheels with semi-pneumatics. All the mechanical drive parts belonging to the Royal Italian Army were fitted with semi-pneumatic elektron

▲ Italian battery in the defence of Rome; in the area of Porta San Paolo the 100/22 were deployed in the first phase to counter the German offensive on the capital with moderate success.

wheels. The shield, shooting seats, ploughshare and towing eye were attached to the shaft. The shield, consisting of a lower element and two upper hinged elements, was equipped with a window and a firing slot, protected by hatches for the aiming systems; two servant seats were attached to the sides of the gun. The gun mount supported the trunnions to which the cradle was attached by means of two vertical sheet metal sides. In addition, two fork arms were attached to the gun mount to support the cradle balancers. The cradle supported the muzzle during the recoil and return movement. The two trunnions on which the muzzle was pivoted were integral with the cradle and regulated by the cogwheel elevation device. Attached to the right trunnion was the recoil adjustment device, which automatically varied the length of the recoil according to the inclination of the muzzle.

The adjustable recoil device allowed very wide vertical sectors of fire, although the shaft was single-tailed.

Pointing was by drum with a panoramic scope.

The ammunition was of the cartridge case type, with the projectile separated from the firing charge, which was contained in a brass case.

▲ France, June 1940. Some Alpine soldiers accompany a 100/22 towed by an old Pavesi. Above, an Italian battery of 100/22 howitzers in action against the Tito partisans in the Balkans.

▲ 100/22 howitzer preserved in the Bari military shrine. Wikipedia.

▼ 100/22 howitzer towed by a FIAT Spa 37 tractor on the African front. Note the curious camouflage applied to the piece.

ITALIAN ARTILLERY 1914-1945

104/32 CANNON AUSTRO-HUNGARIAN WAR BOOTY - EUROPEAN THEATRE 1940-1945

104 CANNON THEN 105/32

The **10.4 cm Feldkanone** or **Fernkampfgeschütz M. 15** was a cannon produced in Austria-Hungary by Škoda and used by the Imperial Army mainly during the First World War. When the Austro-Hungarian Empire disintegrated following the First World War, many of these pieces were requisitioned by the Italian army as compensation. It was then employed as corps artillery by the Regio Esercito during the Ethiopian War of 1935-36, and then during the Second World War, initially referred to as the '104/32 Cannon' and, after 1938, as the '105/32 Cannon'. After the armistice of 8 September 1943, the cannon still remained operational and was used by the artillery of the 10th MAS, while the Wehrmacht took over most of the pieces of the Regio Esercito renaming them *10.5 cm Kanone 320(i)*.

■ EMPLOYMENT IN THE ROYAL ARMY

The several hundred pieces captured by the Italians after the Battle of Vittorio Veneto along with all the others ceded as war reparations to the Kingdom of Italy were, as mentioned, renamed the 104/32 Cannon, where the 32 indicated the length of the barrel expressed in calibre. The original 104 mm piece was then used in 1935 during the Ethiopian War. Then, in 1938, the General Staff decided to increase the calibre of the piece to 105 mm so that it could easily be used with standard Italian ammunition. This operation was carried out by AREN, the Royal Army Arsenal in Naples. In total, some 238 pieces were modified in this way, and they were renamed the **105/32 Cannon** and eventually assigned to the 12 corps artillery groups.

At the outbreak of war, the groups were again sent to Italian East Africa (one battery) and then to the Balkans and Yugoslavia. In Russia, six artillery groups armed with these pieces were created and the pieces were assigned and divided between the 11th and 30th Army Corps Artillery Regiment; in North Africa, more precisely in Tunisia, 35 pieces were assigned to the 30th Army Corps; in June 1943, the gun was still equipping the LIV, LV, LVI and LXIII Army Corps Artillery Group, some of which were then engaged in

▲ A 104 mm Fernkampfgeschütz, an Austrian howitzer version in use during the Great War.

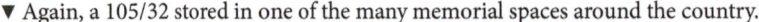

▲ A 105/32 in Tunisia with its gunners ready to fire (courtesy USSM).

▼ Again, a 105/32 stored in one of the many memorial spaces around the country.

coastal defence in Sicily. After the armistice, four 105/32 guns were used on the Anzio-Nettuno front by the 2nd Battery "Lightning" of the Mountain Artillery Group "San Giorgio" of the 3rd Artillery Regiment "Condottieri", a unit of the 10th MAS Flotilla. Others, as mentioned, were instead used by the Wehrmacht.

■ TECHNICAL FEATURES

The cannon's muzzle was made of steel, with the core tube encircled by two reinforcing sleeves and, with its horizontally closing wedge-shaped bolt, weighed 1270 kg. It was encased on a long constant-recoil gun mount, with a double-cone firing brake and a snail sleeve and hydropneumatic retriever for recoil. The gun mount was of the one-tailed type; it was moved by two 130 cm diameter wheels on 12 spokes, on an elastic suspension hall that allowed the gun mount an elevation of -10° to +30° and a swing of 6°; the gun was equipped with a shield and two seats for the servants. The ammunition was of the cartridge-projector type with a metal case.

The towing could be either animal on 3 pairs of horses or mechanical, thanks to a Pavesi tractor. The mechanical transport required two cars, one called a 2850 kg cannon car and a second called a 2750 kg car.

For towing in the mountains, special bogies were used, with a track width of only 950 millimetres, dividing the cannon into *cannon bogie, cradle bogie and hall* and *shield bogie*.

Despite the fact that the 105/32 had the longest range of all the corps artillery in service in the Royal Army between 1940 and 1943, the performance of this weapon was decidedly disappointing and insufficient. Indeed, for similar firepower to the 105/28 gun, the 105/32 was heavier and less manoeuvrable than its counterpart. The towing problems on the mud of the Ukraine were such that the CSIR urgently and in vain demanded its replacement with the 105/28.

The cannon in the course of its history was employed by the following countries:

- Austria-Hungary
- Italy
- Germany
- Yugoslavia
- Romania and Hungary.

TECHNICAL DATA:	
Entry into service	1914 in Italy in 1918
Withdrawal from service	1945
Weight in battery	3299 kg (with shield)
Projectile weight	15-17,5 kg
Total length	3,640 m
Weight of cannon with bolt only	1270 kg
Initial projectile speed	685 m/sec
Horizontal firing sector	5°
Vertical firing sector	-10° / +30°
Maximum range	12.700 m
Rate of fire	min 4/5, max 10 per minute
Number of pieces available in 1942	577
Ammunition 1938 104 grenade	Weight 17,5 kg
" 104 grenade-shrapnel with lead balls	Weight 17,5 kg
" " original	Weight 17,0 kg
" " con irons balls	Weight 15,2 kg

149/12 CANNON MOD. 14 - SPANISH THEATRE 1936-1939

149/12 HOWITZER MOD. 14

The **149/12 howitzer Mod. 14** was a howitzer in use in the German Empire, built by Krupp under the name 15 cm sFH 13. It was produced in Italy under licence by Ansaldo and Vickers-Terni. Assigned to army corps artillery, it was used during the First and Second World Wars and also during the Spanish Civil War.

■ EMPLOYMENT IN THE ROYAL ARMY

Already in 1904, the Imperial German Army had introduced into service the 15 cm sFH 02 howitzer, which was to become the standard German heavy field artillery during the Great War. From this excellent piece, Krupp also derived the 15 cm M. 1906, this one destined for international export, given the good reputation of Krupp products. The howitzer attracted a lot of interest and was bought by the following countries: Bulgaria, the Ottoman Empire, Japan and others. In 1913 a new version, the Krupp 15 cm M. 1913, was produced and this specific model was also purchased in 1914 by the Kingdom of Italy.

With the outbreak of the First World War, and Italy's subsequent entry into the war in 1915, against the Central Empires, Krupp production for Italy naturally came to a halt after delivering 112 pieces. Fortunately for Italy, before the diplomatic crisis took place, Ansaldo and Vickers-Terni had acquired the formal licence to produce the howitzer, which was renamed according to Italian classification to *149/12 howitzer* (where 12 is the length of the barrel expressed in calibre) or also *149/12 A howitzer* (Ansaldo). This excellent piece ended up being produced in over 1,500 examples. In addition to the original Mod. 14, the two Italian companies also produced the **Mod. 16** mountain gun and the **Mod. 18** with a modified barrel. Widely used during the First World War, it was supplied to Albania, then a satellite state of the Kingdom, Bulgaria and probably Austria and Poland. In 1940, Italy entered the war again with 580 Mod. 14 and 116 Mod. 18, having not completed the replacement of this piece with the Škoda 15 cm Vz. 1914 of wartime prey.

▲ Un 149/12 Mod. 14: artiglieri italiani azionano il pezzo sotto la vista del principe Amedeo, Duca d'Aosta, durante la terza battaglia dell'Isonzo, 1915.

149/12 CANNON MOD. 14 - NORTH AFRICAN THEATRE 1940-1945

TECHNICAL FEATURES

The barrel was equipped with a complex 36-relief rifling, usually reinforced by a sleeve carrying the horizontal wedge bolt and a ring about 5 centimetres from the muzzle. The rifle is easily recognisable by the distinctive stepped appearance of the barrel, allowing it to stand out from, for example, its 'brother' Škoda 15 cm Vz. 1914. The sleeve and ring are part of the slide on which the barrel rests. The slide embraces the cradle, on which it slides by means of two side rails; in the cradle are located the central counter-stem and groove firing brake in the cylinder, and the hydropneumatic recuperator, accessible via the characteristic front plate.

The cradle was hinged on the shaft on heavily retracted trunnions. The aiming system consisted of a drum elevator and a panoramic telescope supplied by Cortese-Falcone. The first model, the **Mod. 14**, mounted the original curved shield, fixed at room level. The shaft had a track width of 1.48 m and wooden spoked wheels with a diameter of 1.3 m, with a single tail.

The **Mod. 16**, on the other hand, had a coachwork specially designed by Ansaldo for use in mountainous terrain, with a track width reduced to 1.23 m and wheels with a radius of just one metre; the two wheel halls also had two housings on each side in the shaft: in the normal position, the halls were inserted in the upper housing (height from the ground: 1030 mm), allowing an elevation between 0° and 45°; inserted in the lower housings, they allowed a greater distance from the ground (1060 mm) and the possibility of recoil at elevations between +25° and °65°, allowing positions on mountain slopes to be easily beaten. The firing brake was hydraulic counter-rod with a return valve and spring-loaded retriever.

The last model, the **Mod. 18** was produced in considerable quantities and was distinguished by the curved shield in front of the wheels and the pair of servant seats placed on the tail in the direction of travel. The lift ranged from +3°30' to +65° and the track width increased to 1.50 m. Again, the firing brake was hydraulic counter-rod with a return valve and spring-loaded recuperator.

The towing was done by loading the piece onto an elastic carriage with wheels outside those of the piece, with a track width of 2080 mm and car weight of 2814 kg. Each heavy field howitzer battery consisted of 4 howitzers, 4 Pavesi P4 tractors, 2 machine guns for close defence and 7 trucks. In a running configu-

▲ Field heavy 149/12 howitzer Mod. 1914.

▲ 149/12 howitzers Mod. 14 in Rhodes, visited by Admiral Luigi Biancheri with naval and army officers, 1942.

▼ Another field heavy 149/12 howitzer Mod. 1914 preserved on the Sant'Elia hill.

ration, the battery was 260 m on the road and moved at 12-20 km/h. Setting up the battery usually took only a few minutes.

TECHNICAL DATA:	
	Mod. 1914
Entry into service (in Italy)	1917
Weight in battery	2350 kg
Weight of barrel with bolt	870 kg
Piece length	5,610 m
Barrel length	2,090 m
Bullet Weight	39/42 kg
Total muzzle length	2,250 m
Firing angle	5°
Vertical firing sector	-5° / +43°
Maximum range	6.900 m
Rate of fire	min 3/max, 4 per minute
Number of pieces made	1500

The 149/12 howitzer Mod. 916-918 is the 149/12 howitzer Mod. 916 with the following variants: there is no front ploughshare; the shaft simply rests on the ground and slides on the hall for aiming in the direction. **Main numerical data**: Horizontal firing sector: 5° 20'; Vertical firing sector: +3° 30' +65°; Track width: mm. 1500; Weight of the shaft with shield: kg. 1850.

▲ Beautiful view of the breech of the 149/12 howitzer Mod. 1914. Courtesy Museo della Guerra di Rovereto.

149/35 CANNON MOD. 1901 IN NORTH AFRICA 1940-1945

149/35 CANNON MOD. 1901

The **149/35 Mod. 1901** was a historic cannon used by the Regio Esercito and was one of the first Italian-made steel examples (as it was produced in the Armstrong company's shipyards in Pozzuoli). Named at the time of its adoption, before the Great War, '149 A cannon' (where A stood for 'made of steel'), it was used both on a siege mount, rigid and rotated, and in fixed installations in armoured turrets. For the latter, a warp-mounted version called 149/35 A (Armstrong) was made. The 149/35 was one of the longest-lived and oldest guns still in service until the end of the war.

■ HISTORY AND DESIGN

The design of the cannon dates back as far as 1890; it was conceived as an improvement on the previous 149/23 G (Cast Iron) cannon, which was deemed insufficient and outdated. With the new cannon, the idea was to have a piece capable of an ideal range to accompany the 210/8 D.S. mortar, which, together, formed the backbone of the army artillery.

At that time, other projects concerning field and mountain pieces were under consideration, including the 70 A. Incredible as it may seem, twenty years of studies led to nothing more than a simple rigid carriage (for both the 149 and 70), effectively abandoning the modern warp carriage due to all kinds of difficulties, mainly technical and economic.

The first prototype, made by the Arsenal Regio Esercito di Torino (ARET), was unveiled in 1896 and the first firing trials using an experimental battery took place in 1899. However, by the time it was registered for duty in 1901, the gun, then named 149A, was already old. The enormous mass and weight of over 8 tonnes made it very complicated and difficult, after each firing, to re-set the entire assembly by hand, with the consequent repetition of all the aiming operations, which were also complicated by the fact that

▲ A 149/35 cannon rendered unusable, photographed next to an Austrian soldier at Monfalcone in May 1918.

149/35 CANNON MOD. 1901 - EUROPEAN AND NATIONAL THEATRE 1940-1945

the gun carriage was a single-tailed gun, and therefore obviously had no directional adjustment devices, especially the horizontal one, which required the entire staff to move it! In this state, the first to suffer was the firing cadence.

Such a giant also caused an enormous recoil, even of several metres; completely cancelling the recoil was, moreover, impossible, as it would have caused friction in the trunnions, the whole shaft and the elevating screw, thus irreparably ruining the whole system. They then resorted to wooden pegs and wedges that would naturally reduce the displacement and mechanically return the piece as far as possible to its primitive position.

By contrast, the 149/35 had enviable ballistics. Appreciated above all for its firepower and accuracy, a little less so for its range (less than 18 km), when foreign calibre peers, most of which were equipped with a deformation shaft, fired at least 19-20 km.

Finally in 1911, also thanks to the active collaboration of the German company Krupp, a new and practical cradle and recoil system for the barrel alone was adopted. In early 1915, the final designs were approved, but the entry of the Kingdom of Italy into the war against the Central Empires caused orders for the new pieces to be cancelled.

The Royal Army, forced by the loss of collaboration with Krupp, faced the entire First World War with the 'old' piece. Not only that, in 1917 it was even forced to resume production, simple and cheap. Thus, in 1918, the Regio Esercito still had as many as 598 pieces available.

Due to the economic and social difficulties of the post-war period, it was not until 1922 that the pre-war plans were resumed by the Royal Army Arsenal of Naples (AREN) to modernise this old cannon as much as possible, but the project was discarded; the only significant modification consisted of the application of elastic bogies that would allow mechanical towing at a somewhat higher speed than before.

▲ A 149/35 excellently preserved and displayed on the esplanade in front of the Redipuglia steps.

▲ Beautiful picture of 'apparent' 149/35 during the Abyssinian War in 1935/36. The Pavesi tractor, which was used to tow it, is also clearly visible. Author's collection.

■ EMPLOYMENT IN THE ROYAL ARMY

The 149/35 cannon, despite its age, was widely used during the two world wars. In the Great War, many pieces were lost during the retreat from Caporetto, but the gaps were soon filled before the battle of Vittorio Veneto.

Between 1920 and 1930, only six pieces were sent to Spain with the Volunteer Troops Corps during the Civil War. It is also thought that the piece was not present in Ethiopia, but some photos would seem to confirm otherwise. Most of the pieces, therefore, were intended to operate in the artillery groupings of the Guard at the Frontier (GaF).

When Italy entered the war in June 1940, there were around 60 batteries at the disposal of the border units; in total, there were no less than 870 cannons, of which 28 were specially installed in armoured turrets. The 149/35 cannons placed in the forts of the Alps (in particular those in charge of the Chaberton battery) intervened against the French troops during the Battle of the Western Alps, but more often than not, the use of conventional non-piercing shells failed to pierce the transalpine fortifications. Also framed in the GaF, several pieces operated against Greece and Yugoslavia, where some seventy pieces were active.

As the planned deployment of the Ansaldo 149/40 Mod. 1935, intended to replace the Mod. 1901, was far from complete, the old late 19th century gun was still in the charge of the Army Artillery in 1940. Numerous batteries were then also deployed in Libya, totalling 48 guns of the 5th Army Artillery Regiment and 37 belonging to the GaF, and deployed mainly as defence of the most important strongholds (Tobruch, Bardia, Tripoli).

In January 1942, there were still 46 guns available and at least 16 took part in the desperate defence of Tunisia from February 1943 onwards, despite the numerous reversals and the constant shifting of the front line; sometimes they were so fast, as during Operation Compass, that the British did not even have time to recover the abandoned guns (which were insignificant to them as they were equipped with calibres different from their own standards) or to tamper with them, so that the Italian artillerymen found them exactly where they belonged.

As far as the motherland was concerned, the 149/35 gun was mainly used as artillery for coastal defence, such as in Sicily (it played a similar role in Albania, France, Greece, Dalmatia and the Italian Dodecanese), for a total of 16 fully armed and efficient groups as of June 1943.

■ TECHNICAL FEATURES

The barrel was steel, with rifling of 48 lines or a mixture of 36 lines, an absolute novelty at the time!
The diameter/barrel at the muzzle was 149 mm and, despite the name 35, the actual length of the barrel was enormous, some 5.5 metres. This feature was due to a later modification of the barrel compared to the first examples put into circulation without any change to the name; on the outside of the breech there was a rim which also carried the trunnions for positioning the muzzle. The breech-closing device consisted of a classic cylindrical bolt (without rifling) with three manoeuvres and a plastic ring hermetic closure, while the primer was a friction-filled blowpipe.
The 'siege' shaft, a rigid one-tailed steel type with a footboard for the servants, was wheeled with wooden spokes of 1560 mm diameter and 1480 mm track. Elevation was adjusted by means of a handwheel on the tail of the shaft, the gears of which acted on a toothed sector connected to the breech. As an aiming device, the piece was equipped with a Mod. Cortese rifle sight.
To facilitate towing and to contain recoil, the characteristic 'caterpillar tracks' patented by Italian Captain Crispino Bonagente were installed on the wheel treads in the pre-war years. Visible in almost all photographs of artillery pieces of many nations involved in the Great War, the 'Bonagente' tracks were formed by 12 rectangular plates joined by 12 elements on each wheel, which widened the wheel bearing surface allowing transit over soft and yielding terrain and above all making the use of the heavy wooden

▲ The incredible and archaic line of the old 149/35 used on the Tunisian front. Just think of the technical comparison with a German 88 piece used by the Afrika Korps. NARA collection.

ITALIAN ARTILLERY 1914-1945

platforms (called paioli), on which siege artillery was placed in battery, unnecessary. Other equipment was provided by the wedges and the bench.

The wedges were two inclined planes, larger than those used with the platform, which were placed about one and a half metres behind the wheels. At the moment of firing, the cannon recoiled on the two wedges, which, thanks to its weight, slowed down its travel, after which the cannon, by gravity, returned to its starting position. The belly was a sort of wooden and metal sled positioned under the tail of the gunstock; it accompanied the tail in recoil, preventing, together with the wedges, the misalignment of the piece; at the same time, by friction, it braked its retrograde travel.

Mechanical towing (using a Pavesi-Tolotti Type B or Breda TP32 tractor) was carried out by means of a front-mounted tractor, after the barrel had been set back on special supports placed on the tail of the shaft, so as to shift the centre of gravity backwards. On longer routes, another method was used: the piece was broken down by loading the barrel onto a tractor-trailer and the shaft onto another truck-drawn trailer.

The 149/35 Mod. 1901 battery consisted, in the 1930s, of 4 cannons, 4 artillery tractors, 10 trucks, 10 trailers and 2 machine guns for close defence of the piece. On the road, the battery extended about 400 metres and moved at 6-8 km/h.

TECHNICAL DATA:	
Entry into service	1901
Weight in battery	8.600 kg
Projectile weight	From 36 to 42 kg
Initial projectile speed	628 m/sec
Firing angle	0°
Vertical firing sector	-10° / +35°
Maximum range	15.500 m
Rate of fire	1 shot every 6 minutes
Number of pieces available in 1940	923

▲ Italian 149/35 and 120/25 cannon battery captured by the British during the 1940-1941 winter offensive in Cyrenaica. NARA collection.

152/37 HOWITZER

The **Škoda 15 cm Vz. 15/16** also known as the **15 cm Autokanone M. 15/16** was a large gun produced by Austria-Hungary and used during the First World War. After the war was lost, some pieces (29 to be precise) were given to the Kingdom of Italy as war reparations. In Italy, the piece was renamed as the '152/37 Cannon'. The Royal Army made extensive use of it, first during the Spanish Civil War and then during the Second World War. Germany also used the pieces captured from Austria after the Anschluss and from Czechoslovakia after the occupation on the Atlantic Wall in a fixed position, renaming them as *15.2 cm K 15/16(t)*, while the pieces captured from the Regio Esercito after 8 September were referred to as *15.2 cm K 410(i)*.

EMPLOYMENT IN THE ROYAL ARMY

This heavy cannon made by Škoda during the First World War had two versions: the first, the Vz. 15 (or Model 15), dating from 1915, had wooden wheels and limited 30° elevation and was produced in 27 examples; the following year the improved Vz. 15/16 with metal wheels and increased lift to 45°, as required by specifications for mountain use.
The Regio Esercito obtained some 30 pieces out of a total of 44 produced by Austria-Hungary. These were all overhauled in 1920 by the Royal Army Arsenal in Naples (AREN) and brought up to the Mod. 15/16 standard. Thus upgraded, they took part in the Spanish adventure in 1935/36 with the Volunteer Troops Corps. In June 1940 they were then employed in the offensive against France.
The 152/37 equipped the 131st and 132nd Batteries of the LI Army Artillery Group in Greece and Yugoslavia, as well as the 134th and 135th of the LII Army Artillery Group sent to the Libyan front.
In June 1943, the only group of 152/37 still operational was the LIV of the 5th Army, while the remaining pieces had been downgraded from heavy army artillery to coastal artillery.
Thus, the guns of the 133rd and 134th Batteries of the LIII Group joined the Coastal Defence from Position.

▲ 15 cm howitzer vz. 15/16 Skoda in service with the Austro-Hungarian forces in 1917.

152/37 HOWITZER - EUROPEAN AND NATIONAL THEATRE 1940-1945

■ TECHNICAL FEATURES

The *Vz. 15/16* was one of the first Austrian heavy pieces expressly designed for mechanical towing, so much so that it was also called the **15 cm Autokanone M. 15/16**.

Also modern was the steel barrel, consisting of a 42-ribbed right-hand rifled core, rimmed by two sleeves, of which the rear one carried a horizontal wedge, for a total weight of 4780 kg. It was mounted on an elastic, hydro-pneumatic firing-brake and recuperator (for the return to battery), which in turn was encased on a traditional two-wheeled, single-tailed, elastically-suspended shaft. On either side of the tail, on two special seats, two servants took their places during towing. The shaft of the Mod. 15 allowed an elevation of 30°, which was negative and considered insufficient; due to this fact it was later increased to 45° on the Italian Mod. 15/16, while the swing remained limited to 6°, also unfortunately not optimal. Originally, Austrian mounts were equipped with a wide shield (see photo at the beginning of the chapter), later removed on Italian pieces.

The towing was mechanical and was carried out in two cars: the cannon was dug in and transported on a special cannon carriage, while the second car was the gun carriage with a front end.

The two cars weighed 8495 and 9200 kg respectively and were towed by heavy artillery tractors such as the Breda TP32. Alternatively, the two sections were loaded onto two Viberti trailers pulled by Lancia 3Ro trucks.

The battery consisted of:

- 4 cannons;
- 8 ammunition trailers (or trucks);
- 2 machine guns for close defence;
- 1 powder wagon;
- 5 support trucks.

It moved at a speed of 8-10 km/h, covering a length of 600 metres. Commissioning took about three hours.

▲ A 152/37 howitzer in battery with its entire crew engaged in firing. State Archives.

152/37 HOWITZER - NORTH AFRICA THEATRE 1940-1943

TECHNICAL DATA:	
Entry into service	1915
Weight in battery	11.900 kg
Length	9,850 m
Barrel length	6,000 m
Bullet Weight	47/ 56 kg
Initial projectile speed	692 m/sec
Firing angle	6°
Vertical firing range	-6° / +45°
Maximum range	21.800 m
Rate of fire	1 shot every two minutes
Number of pieces available in 1940	29 to Italy (44 in total originally)

The weapon served the following countries: Austria-Hungary, Italy, Germany, Austria, Czechoslovakia.

▲ Details of 152/37 howitzer.

152/37 HOWITZER ON VIBERTI TRANSPORT - NORTH AFRICA THEATRE 1940-1943

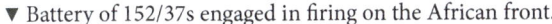

▲ 152/37 howitzer loaded onto a Viberti transport and towed by a Lancia RO truck.

▼ Battery of 152/37s engaged in firing on the African front.

ITALIAN ARTILLERY 1914-1945

210/8 D.S. MORTAR - EUROPEAN AND NATIONAL THEATRE 1915-1945

210/8 D.S. MORTAR

The **210/8 D.S. mortar**, also referred to as a heavy siege mortar, equipped the Royal Italian Army and the Polish Army from its inception to the end of the war in 1945. This piece was developed by Ansaldo in the last years of the 19th century as a mortar for siege artillery, thus intended, according to the tactics of the time, for static use against fortresses and heavily protected targets.

In 1900 it entered the Royal Army's siege fleet by right. Massively employed throughout the course of the Great War and throughout the Second World War, partly due to its size, partly due to obsolescence, and partly due to changing tactics, these heavy mortars never left Italy (except for a few units destined for the Dodecanese islands) and were mainly employed by the Frontier Guard units in the Alpine Wall fortifications. Also acquired by the Polish army, it was employed by the latter against the Russians in the Soviet-Polish war of 1919.

The 210/8 D.S. mortar is named after the type of shaft used, the so-called 'De Stefano' model. The same mortar also existed on an earlier, simpler type of installation, known as the 'De Angelis' model (210/8 D.A.) and one on a platform (210/8 PIAT.).

OTHER VERSIONS

210/8 PIAT. mortar: the firing mouth and ammunition remain the same, but the installation is on a platform. The box-type barrel rests on the sub-staff with sloping rails, which is braked by two hydraulic brakes. The sub-bust is pivoted on a platform of oak beams and stringers. The elevation ranges from -15° to +60° with useful firing elevation starting at 40°, while the firing sector is limited to 30°. The weight of the installation (carriage, undercarriage and platform, without firing port) is 5.430 t.

▲ 210 mortar battery at the front during the First World War in Val Dogna. Author's colouring.

▲ Italian artillery at Ventimiglia (June 1940). 210/8 mortar in action during the Battle of the Western Alps.

▼ 210/8 mortar also deployed on the Alpine front in 1940.

This version was towed by three cars:
- mortar car, equipped with salt and wheels, weighing 4.139 t and towed on the front.
- under-body transport wagon, weighing 2,880 t.
- platform transport wagon, weighing 2.9 t with front axle.

Mortar 210/8 D.A.: the 'De Angelis' type installation consists of an under-body with hydraulic brakes resting on a platform. It differs from the PIAT. type in the presence of removable jacks with wheels at the four corners of the platform that allow rotation over a 90° sector on a circular rail, fixed to a wooden scaffold. The towing for this mortar is done in the same way as for the PIAT version.

■ TECHNICAL FEATURES

The barrel, 2048 mm long with 36 right-hand stripes, was made of steel with a layer of rim around the breech. The bolt was of the screw type. The muzzle thus composed weighed a total of 2.1 t and in this form remained unchanged in the various installations.

The 'De Stefano' barrel is a case with a plain sub-barrel. Specifically, the barrel is encased on a slide, which slides on smooth bars (rails) inclined upwards at the rear. When fired, the muzzle recoils on the smooth-bore, braked by two hydraulic cylinders at the front, and then automatically returns to the battery thanks to the inclination of the slide bed. The under-battery itself, on four wheels with a front wheel, recoils simultaneously on two rails in two elements each, joined by crossbars and resting on a layer of beams that transfers the effort to the ground, which has previously been perfectly levelled. The total weight of the complex is 8.830 t. The elevation ranges from -15° to +70° with useful shooting elevation from 35°, while the shooting sector of the shaft on the platform is 360°.

Loading is by means of a bucket with a hoist, while the firing of the projectile and launching charges is manual, (as can be clearly seen in the adjacent photo). The normal firing rate is 1 shot every 7-8 minutes, the maximum rate is 2 shots every 5 minutes.

The towing unit consists of a car made up of a shaft and mortar; wheels fitted with caterpillar tracks are mounted on the underframe and it is joined to a front end, also with caterpillar tracks. The complex reaches a weight of 5.7 tonnes. For towing in the mountains, however, the piece is broken down, the mortar being towed on a special cart, while the shaft is towed on its forecarriage.

The siege battery consists of 4 mortars, 4 trailers, 2 machine guns for close-range defence, 1 truck for transporting the firing charges and 4 trucks for the shells. In running configuration, the battery is 420 m on the road and moves at 6 to 8 km/h. Battery deployment takes 6 to 8 hours.

TECHNICAL DATA:	
Entry into service	1900
Weight in battery	10.930 kg
Barrel length	2,048 m
Height to the knee	1,5 m
Withdrawal from service	1945
Projectile weight	61/103 kg
Initial bullet velocity	370 m/sec
Firing angle	360°
Vertical field of fire	-15° / +70°
Maximum range	8.000 m
Rate of fire	1 shot every 7-8 minutes
Ammunition	210 grenade weighing 100 kg 210 cast-iron grenade weighing 102 kg 210 grenade-bomb weighing 61.4 kg

▲▼ In these two pictures, taken by the Austrian engineers, two 210 mortars partially disassembled and stored in a depot or on site. They have the merit of charmingly showing the shape of this artillery piece.

240 BOMBARD

The **240 mm bombard** was a bombard derived from the French Mortier de 240 mm and used by the Royal Italian Army and other armies such as the Russian, American, British, Austrian, German and of course French armies during the First World War.

■ PROJECT HISTORY

The trench mortar was produced in a short-barrelled version *'CT Mle 1915'* and later with an extended barrel, called *'240 LT Mle 1916'*. The weapon was purchased in both versions by the Royal Army when the Kingdom of Italy had not yet entered the war in the First World War.

The two national versions were respectively named *'Bombarda da 240 C'* and *'Bombarda da 240 L'* and produced under licence by Vickers-Terni. In particular, the latter was by far the most produced and used on the Italian front, renamed during the First World War as the *'240/12 Bombarda'*. A third version was

▲ Italian 240 mm bombard.

made with a barrel that could be lengthened if necessary by adding a section of tube, bolted to the muzzle.

In February 1916, the Ministry of War set up a new speciality of the Artillery Corps specifically for this new type of weapon, called the Bomber Corps, with multi-armour groups equipped with 240 L, 240 C and 58 bombards. The 240 mm battery, based on 4 sections of 2 guns each had a staff of 7 officers, 215 troops, 62 quadrupeds, 8 bombards, a baggage wagon, 26 battalion carriages and 4 bicycles and was placed under the command of an artillery or cavalry captain. At the end of 1916, as many as 510 240 mm bombards were in service in the Regio Esercito.

Between the two wars, some 240/12 bombers, considered obsolete, were ceded to Montenegro. However, when Italy entered World War II in 1940, 334 pieces were still in the arsenals of the Regio Esercito; these were all deployed to the Guard on the border with France and Yugoslavia.

■ TECHNICAL FEATURES

The barrel was encased on a rigid shaft, with a cogged device for elevation and a pivot pin that allowed it to swing in all directions. The barrel was of the smoothbore type. The shaft rotated on a metal platform resting on a cauldron of wooden beams. The 67-kilogram bomb, with about 30 kilograms of explosive charge, equipped with stabilising fins, was inserted into the barrel from the muzzle, while the ballistite launch charge was loaded from the breech box. The range, approximately 1 km for the C version, increased to 2 km in the L and A versions.

▲ Italian 240 mm bombard placed on the Adamello glaciers, 1915-18.

TECHNICAL DATA:	
Entry into service	1915
Weight in battery	866 kg
Barrel length	CT 1,92 m, LT 3,05 m
Withdrawal from service	1945
Projectile weight	67/81 kg
Initial bullet velocity	145 m/sec
Firing angle	36°
Vertical firing range	+54° / +75°
Maximum range	2.000 m
Shooting speed	1 shot every 6 minutes

▲ Italian 240 mm bombard reused by the Austrians on the Piave front, 1917-1918.

260/9 MORTAR MOD. 16 - EUROPEAN AND NATIONAL THEATRE 1915-1945

260/9 MORTAR MOD. 16

The **260/9 mortar Model 16** was an Italian heavy mortar and siege gun, designed by the French Schneider and produced under licence in Italy by Ansaldo and Vickers-Terni for the Italian Army. It was used by the Italian Army during both World War I and World War II.

■ PROJECT HISTORY

After the independence and unification of Italy, the Italians had fallen far behind in arms design and production. Foreign companies such as Armstrong, Krupp, Schneider and Vickers took advantage of this national industrial absence and supplied weapons or reached agreements to allow local production of their designs under licence.

Although most of the belligerent powers in 1914 had heavy field artillery before the outbreak of the First World War, none of them could boast an adequate number of heavy guns in service. Not only that, no one had even thought about the importance that this branch of artillery would play in the course of the conflict. Every country, at first, was forced to scrape the barrel in search of these heavy cannons. Forts, armouries, coastal forts and even museums were scoured in search of this type of artillery to be sent straight to the front.

Special transport systems (mechanical and rail) were also built for these cannons, in order to speed up the supply of adequate weapons to hit trenches and concrete fortifications of the enemy as much as possible.

■ TECHNICAL FEATURES

260/9 S mortar: this was the original name of the Schneider model supplied to the Italian Army. It had a steel box slide, a recoil spade, two wooden spoked wheels with steel rims, a shield, a hydropneumatic recoil mechanism and a Schneider interrupted screw breech. It fired separate cased ammunition with up to eight rounds per bag to vary velocity and range. The firing slide had a large hollow section near the breech to allow high-angle fire and, as with all other large Schneider guns, had a convenient loading

▲ Italian 260/9 mm mortar captured by the Austrians at San Giovanni on 1 November 1917.

260/9 MORTAR MOD. 16 - EUROPEAN AND NATIONAL THEATRE 1915-1945

tray integrated into the breech. The combat weight was 12147 kg and it could be broken down into two carriages for transport. The barrel could be removed and moved on its own 5660 kg carriage, while the second 6970 kg carriage consisted of the carriage and a mechanism to support the carriage tail. On the carriage, translation was only 6°. Although the Italian classification indicates that the mortar was 9-calibre, in reality it was 10.5 calibre. The Italian classification system in fact did not count the breech length as most other countries did.

260/9 mortar Model 16: this was the simplified design built in Italy under licence in 1916. The gun barrel was the same, but in action the wheels were removed and the carriage formed a kind of firing platform. The mortar could be transported in one piece and a detachable set of wooden spoke wheels with steel rims could be mounted on the front of the carriage. The barrel could also be retracted backwards and laid on top of the carriage for transport. The tail of the carriage was then supported in turn by a limb for towing. The movement speed of the piece was 6-8 km/h and the time required to set up the mortar in battery was as much as 24 hours. The translation of the carriage was then increased to 12°, but the performance of the piece remained unchanged.

The organisation of this type of mortar battery consisted of: 4 mortars, 4 trailers, 2 machine guns, 1 multi-purpose truck, 4 trucks.

TECHNICAL DATA:	
Entry into service	1910 France, 1916 Italy
Weight in battery	28.500 kg
Length	5,6 m
Projectile weight	215-223 kg
Initial projectile speed	350 m/sec
Firing angle	12°
Vertical field of fire	+20° / +65°
Maximum range	9.100 m
Shooting speed	1 shot every 6 minutes

▲ Italian 260/9 mm mortar in battery in the mountains of Trentino.

305/17 MORTAR

The **305/17 howitzer** was the most powerful artillery weapon in service in the Royal Italian Army during the First World War. It was only retired in 1959!

■ PROJECT HISTORY

In 1908, the Italian Coast Artillery found itself in need of replacing a weapon, the 280 mm Ansaldo howitzer, which was judged to be no longer up to the task. The General Staff then turned to the usual firms (Armstrong, Krupp, Schneider, Saint Chamond and Vickers-Terni) for preliminary designs for a new 305 mm howitzer. The Commission of the General Inspectorate of Artillery eventually chose that of Armstrong-Pozzuoli from the various designs, while formulating some variations and modifications to the ammunition, shielding and loading system. The weapon entered coastal artillery service in 1914 as a **305/17 coastal installation howitzer**, equipping the La Spezia square with 12 pieces, the La Maddalena square in Sardinia with 4 and the Messina square with 4.

With the outbreak of the Great War, the need arose to reinforce the fleet of siege pieces, and therefore various designs for a mobile howitzer for the 305 mm were evaluated. Based on a design by General Garrone, from an initial **305/17 howitzer G. Mod. 1915**, two mechanical towed models were produced, the **305/17 howitzer G. Mod. 1916** and the **305/17 howitzer G. Mod. 1917** (the "G." stands for Garrone). By installing the Mod. 1916's gun tube on the standardised gun carriage designed by De Stefano, the **305/17 D.S. howitzer** was produced.

In October 1917, 38 pieces were thus available in the three versions. After the loss of 9 guns following the Battle of Caporetto, 18 more were produced between 1 July 1918 and 30 June 1919, bringing the total to 44 guns, of which 8 were in reserve. In 1937, during the Spanish Civil War, 5 pieces were finally handed over to the Francoists. In 1939, 10 Mod. 16 and 17 Mod. 17 complexes were in service in the army artillery; at the outbreak of hostilities, these pieces armed the 540th battery of the 22nd Frontier Guard Artillery Group (G.a.F.), one battery of the XXIX and one of the XXXI Group of the 24th Artillery Regiment G.a.F. and the

▲ Italian 305/17 howitzer Mod. 1917 in battery ready to fire.

4th Army Artillery Regiment; these pieces were used in the French campaign at the beginning of the war and in the defence of the port of Naples and the coast of Sicily. A further 16 shafts on a scudded coastal installation were supplied to 4 coastal batteries of the Regia Marina manned by MILMART personnel. Some of the guns remained in service in the post-war period with the newly formed Italian Army, only to be permanently decommissioned in 1959, testifying to the good quality of the piece.

■ TECHNICAL FEATURES

The barrel, made of steel, consisted of a 60-stripe left-handed constant-pitch core and sleeve and band rims; it was 5.881 m long and weighed 1,790 kg with the bolt. The latter was screw-type with continuous operation. The barrel was inserted into the sleeve cradle, which housed the two hydraulic firing brake cylinders and the hydropneumatic retriever cylinder at the top. The cradle was encased on a box-type barrel, with a height at the toggle of 1.43 m and an elevation range of +20° to +65°, resting and rotating 360° on a metal platform. The swing was achieved by lowering the wheels at the four corners of the shaft by means of jacks and manually rotating the shaft, with the help of a rope tied near the muzzle of the barrel. On the left side of the shaft was positioned the loading spoon, on a candlestick support. The platform in turn rested on a caisson sunk into the ground. The weight in battery reached 33770 kg; the maximum range was 17600 m, with an initial projectile speed of 545 m/s. For towing, the gun was broken down into a muzzle, ramrod, platform and caisson. These were loaded onto special wagons and towed by Pavesi-Tolotti tractors and, later, by Breda TP32s:

- *howitzer carriage* weighing 17510 kg; the track width with the tracks installed was 1500 mm;
- *bustle carriage* weighing 14490 kg;
- *platform carriage* weighing 7870 kg;
- *crane tank* to battery the piece, also transporting the caisson and beams, weighing 7840 kg.

The battery consisted of two howitzers with 8 cars, 2 machine guns for close defence, a powder wagon and 5 trucks; the column was 600 metres deep and moved at 6-8 km/h. Setting up the battery took an entire day, due to the deep excavation for the sinking of the pyramid-shaped caisson.

▲ An Italian artilleryman sitting next to two shells from the giant howitzer.

305/17 howitzer G. Mod. 1916: the Mod. 1916 is very similar to the Mod. 1917, differing essentially in the bolt, similar to that of the 305/10, and minor differences in the weight of the trailing lugs.

This version consisted of the Mod. 1916's muzzle, cradle and elastic organs installed on a "De Stefano" carriage; this carriage with smooth-bore underbelly was on four wheels, with a front wheel, and slid on two smooth rails sloping upwards at the rear, joined together and fixed at the front to a platform of beams by a revolving support; rotating the smooth rails on this support, the piece was swung through 360°. The energy of the recoil not absorbed by the firing brake was dissipated by the retrograde movement of the shaft on the smoothbore; the latter being inclined, the piece then returned to the battery by gravity. Loading was done by means of a bucket with a hoist, while the projectile and launching charges were cast by hand. Towing was carried out on a single car; the front axle was fitted with a fifth wheel and, once the track tracks (designed by Major Crispino Bonagente on the four wheels) were installed, towing was carried out directly with the Pavesi-Tolotti artillery tractor.

The 305 howitzer was used by the Royal Italian Army, the Spanish Army and the Army of the Italian Social Republic.

TECHNICAL DATA:	
Entry into service	1914
Withdrawal from service	1959
Weight in battery	33.750 kg
Barrel length	5,88 m
Bullet weight	295-442 kg
Initial bullet velocity	545 m/sec
Angle of fire	360°
Vertical firing range	+20° / +65°
Rate of fire	1 shot every 5/12 minutes
Maximum range	17.600 m
Pieces produced	44

▲ Detail of the Garrone bust, with the wheel jacks and the loading spoon with the projector.

AUTOCARRETTA OM   ITALY 1932-1945

OM AUTOCARRETTA

In order to speed up and improve the connections between the troops in the high mountains and the barracks at the bottom of the valley, a number of light vehicles were designed and put into operation in the early 1930s, such as the 6.5-tonne Lancia 3Ro 4x2, which was also used as a self-propelled anti-aircraft gun, the Fiat-SPA 38R 4x2 and the Fiat Dovunque 33, but the most versatile and most used vehicle was the **Autocarretta OM** (OM motorized carrette). The vehicle was frequently used as an artillery tractor, especially for light pieces.

The first wartime employment took place during the Ethiopian War, and in May 1936, 1337 units were sent to Eritrea and another 78 to Somalia. During the Spanish Civil War, the Volunteer Troops Corps employed 328 units distributed in Autosections of 24 vehicles each, mainly used for the mechanical towing of 65/17 Mod. 1908/1913 cannons.

The Regio Esercito entered the Second World War with 2751 autocarrette (not counting those in Italian East Africa) and other commissioned ones. Despite the difficulties encountered with the Model 36 DM and P autocarrette, these were used extensively throughout the conflict, especially on the Russian front and in the Balkans. On the Balkan theatre of operations, it was also used on narrow-gauge lines, equipped with makeshift armour consisting of small trench shields dating back to the First World War, and with pneumatic wheels replaced by railway wheels. Production was discontinued in favour of the more modern SPA CL39 and Fiat-SPA 38R light trucks, while the designated replacement, the Pavesi R.8, although undergoing technical trials since 1936, never went into production.

TECHNICAL DATA:	
Entry into service	1932
Weight at full load	1.615 kg
Chassis length	3,8 m
Power	20/23 hp
Engine	1616 cm^3 4-cylinder petrol
Vehicle width	1,3 m
Maximum speed	20/40 km/h
Autonomy	160 km
Number of parts available in 1940	A few thousand

■ TECHNICAL FEATURES

The mechanical part ranged from 20 hp of the Mod. 32 to 23 hp of later models, and a maximum speed of 20 km/h for the first model and 40 km/h in later models. The OM truck was equipped with double transverse leaf spring suspension and 4-wheel steering with semi-pneumatic tyres (with possible tracks), in the first models, or pneumatic tyres in the later versions. This vehicle, very versatile and with good mechanical qualities, was able to overcome the steepest stretches of high mountain military roads (a good example is the Val Morino military road, which leads from Fenils to the Chaberton Battery in a journey of around 14 km and 72 hairpin bends), although its poor stability made it difficult to use on transverse routes. Its proven manoeuvrability and sufficient towing power as mentioned also made it a good light artillery tractor.

▲ An OM 32 engaged in East Africa in 1935.

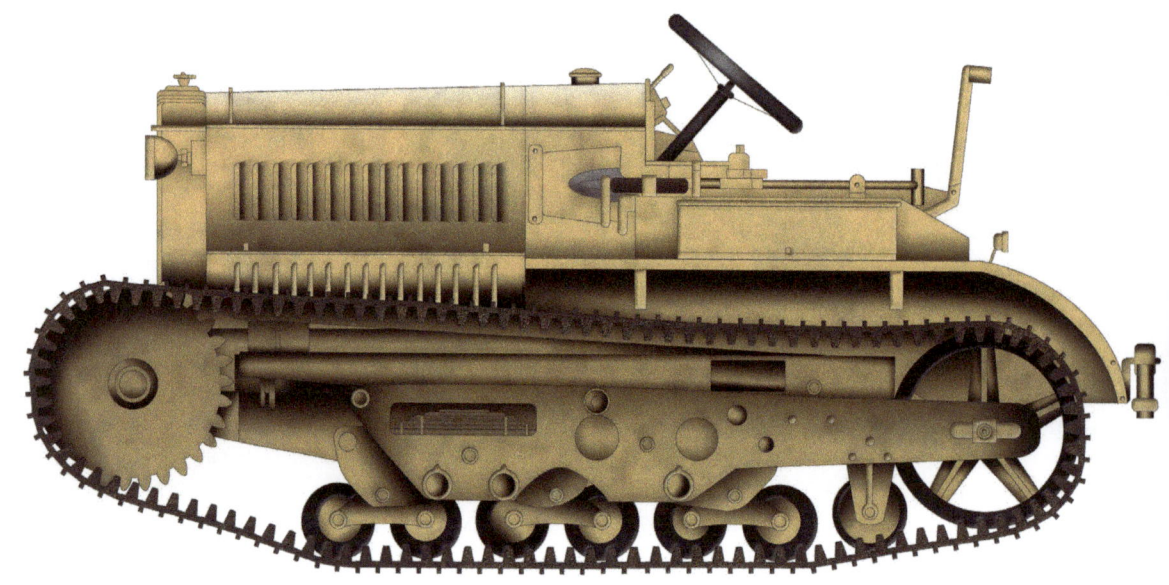

FIAT- OCI 708 CM TRACTOR IN NORTH AFRICA 1940-1943

TRACTOR FIAT- OCI 708 CM IN SPAIN 1935-1936

FIAT 708 TRACTOR

Following the Royal Army's adoption of the 75/18 howitzer, a light artillery tractor was needed to tow the piece and ammunition into the mountains. In 1934, Officine Costruzioni Industriali (OCI) of Modena, a company that actually belonged to the FIAT group, presented a prototype based on the Fiat 708 C agricultural tractor, suitably reinforced and renamed **Fiat-OCI 508 CM**, where the 'M' stands for 'military'. In 1935, an initial batch of 200 vehicles was ordered, designated by the army as the **OCI 708 CM mountain tractor**. The vehicle remained in production until 1943.

It made its operational debut during the Ethiopian War, when it was sent to Eritrea in 1935 with two groups on 77/28 guns. In the same year it equipped the 63rd Infantry Division 'Cyrene' and the 1st CC.NN. "23 March" in Libya, while in 1936 it was deployed to Somalia with the 32nd Autogroup and used in the manoeuvres of the 10th Artillery Regiment "Volturno" for towing 75/18 howitzers.

Fifty-four units took part in the Spanish Civil War, while when Italy entered the war in 1940, 381 tractors were in the 5th Army; by October 1941, only 113 of these remained, most of them in the 102nd Motorised Division 'Trento' and the 5th Airborne Squadron. The tractor had in fact also been adopted by the Regia Aeronautica to move aircraft on the runways. The vehicles that remained in the metropolitan area in 1941 were all transferred to the military engineering depots. Some examples were used after the Cassibile armistice by the forces of the Social Republic.

TECHNICAL DATA:	
Entry into service	1935-36
Weight at full load	2.500kg
Chassis length	3,04 m
Power	30 hp
Displacement	2500
Vehicle width	1,23 m
Maximum speed	16 km/h
Autonomy	140 km
Number of parts available in 1940	About 400

■ TECHNICAL FEATURES

The 708 CM retained the typical layout of the crawler agricultural tractor; in fact, as mentioned, it was derived from the Fiat 708 C, a lightened version of the Fiat 700 C, the first mass-produced crawler tractor in Europe. The engine, unlike its petrol-driven predecessors, was a 2520 cm³ Fiat 308 C petrol engine, delivering 30 hp at 2300 rpm. The steering wheel, offset to the right, activated the steering clutches. The rolling train differs from the 708 C: the toothed drive wheel is at the front and the leaf spring suspension system of the track rollers is reminiscent of that of the M-series wagons.

▲ Detail of the tractor frame.

Excellent off-road, its fragile mechanics penalised it on long journeys, so much so that it was usually transferred to trucks. In addition to its 'institutional' role of towing the 75/18 piece and its 80 ammunition box, it was also used to transport material for infantry divisions. It was successfully tested for towing the 47/32 Mod. 1935, but the experiment was not followed up.

ITALIAN ARTILLERY 1914-1945

BIBLIOGRAPHY

- Balocco R. – *Fanti ed Artiglieri* – Manualetti di Tecnica Militare, Fascicolo XXI, dic. 1934
- Barlozzetti U. & Alberto Pirella *Mezzi dell'Esercito Italiano 1935-45*, Editoriale Olimpia, 1986.
- Benussi G. *Autocannoni, autoblinde e veicoli speciali del Regio Esercito Italiano nella Prima Guerra Mondiale.* Integest Milano 1973.
- Bovi L, Antonio e Andrea Talillo. *Semoventi da 47/32, 90/53 e 75/18 in Sicilia.* Ediz. illustrata - Ardite edizioni 2021. Italia
- Cappellano F. – *Le artiglierie del Regio Esercito nella Seconda Guerra Mondiale*, Albertelli, 1998
- Cappellano F. *Mortai del Regio Esercito* Storia militare agosto 1997
- Ceva L., Curami A. – *La meccanizzazione dell'esercito italiano dalle origini al 1943* – Stato Maggiore Esercito, Ufficio Storico, 1994
- Chiappa E., *CTV - il corpo truppe volontarie italiano durante la guerra civile spagnola*, 2003 EMI.
- COMITATO PER LA STORIA DELL'ARTIGLIERIA, *Storia dell'artiglieria italiana*, vol. XVI, 1955
- Cucut C. - *Le forze armate della RSI* –Gruppo Modellistica Trentino, 2005
- Cucut C. *Le artiglierie delle forze armate della Repubblica sociale italiana.* Soldiershop ottobre 2020
- De Rosa Gabriele *Storia dell'Ansaldo 6. Dall'IRI alla guerra 1930-1945*, Gius. Laterza & Figli, 1999.
- Favagrossa C. – *Perché perdemmo la guerra* – Rizzoli, 1946
- Finazzer E. *Guida alle artiglierie italiane nella Seconda Guerra Mondiale, 1940-1945. Regio Esercito italiano, Repubblica Sociale Italiana, esercito cobelligerante.* IS Genova 2020.
- Finazzer E. *Le Artiglierie del Regio Esercito nella Seconda Guerra Mondiale.* Soldiershop 2017.
- Finazzer E & Riccio R. *Italian Artillery of the Second World War.* Mushroom 2015.
- Grandi F., *Dati sommari sulle artiglierie in servizio e sul tiro*, Ed. fuori commercio, 1934.
- Grandi F., *Le armi e le artiglierie in servizio*, Ed. fuori commercio, 1938.
- Guglielmi Daniele *Semoventi M41 & M42.* Armor Photogallery -Broncos (in inglese)
- Montanari M.– *L'esercito italiano alla vigilia della 2ª Guerra Mondiale* – Stato Maggiore Esercito, Ufficio Storico, 1975
- Pergher C. – *Le macchine di Pavesi* – Gruppo Modellistico Trentino, 2002
- Pignato N. – *L'obice da 149/19 OTO 1937* – Storia Militare n. 150, marzo 2006
- Pignato N. - *Artiglierie e automezzi dell'esercito italiano nella Seconda guerra mondiale.* Albertelli editore 1972
- Pignato N. Cappellano F. – *L'obice da 210/22 Mod. 35* – Storia Militare n. 171, gennaio 2008
- Pignato N. – *Il 105/28 del Regio Esercito* – Storia Militare n. 182, novembre 2008
- Pignato N. – *L'ultimo 75 dell'artiglieria italiana* – Storia Militare n. 188, maggio 2009
- Pignato N. – *Un "pezzo da 90"* – Storia Militare n. 201, giugno 2010
- Pignato, N. *Semovente da 75/18 : tecnica e storia del primo semovente italiano.* (2010).Parma: Albertelli.
- Raudino S. e Stefanelli E. – *Storia dell'artiglieria italiana*, parte V – voll. XV e XVI - Rivista d'artiglieria e genio 1953 - 1955
- Rovighi A. – F. Stefani, *La partecipazione italiana alla guerra civile spagnola*, USSME, 1992.
- Tonoli M. e F. Corsetti *Skodas Gebirgskanone Model 15 1915-1964* – Itinera Progetti (2013).

ALREADY PUBLISHED TITLES

ALL BOOKS IN THE SERIES ARE PRINTED IN ITALIAN AND ENGLISH

VISIT OUR WEBSITE FOR MORE INFORMATION ON THE WEAPONS ENCYCLOPAEDIA:

https://soldiershop.com/collane/libri/the-weapons-encyclopaedia/

TWE-015 EN

www.ingramcontent.com/pod-product-compliance
Lightning Source LLC
LaVergne TN
LVHW072121060526
838201LV00068B/4941